Baby
Animals

BABY KOALAS

Martha E. H. Rustad

Raintree is an imprint of Capstone Global Library Limited, a company incorporated in England and Wales having its registered office at 264 Banbury Road, Oxford, OX2 7DY – Registered company number: 6695582

www.raintree.co.uk
myorders@raintree.co.uk

Edited by Alison Deering
Designed by Jennifer Bergstrom
Original illustrations © Capstone Global Library Limited 2____
Picture research by Tracy Cummins
Production by Tori Abraham
Originated by Capstone Global Library Ltd

978 1 3982 2393 6 (hardback)
978 1 3982 2396 7 (paperback)

British Library Cataloguing in Publication Data
A full catalogue record for this book is available from the British Library.

Acknowledgements
We would like to thank the following for permission to reproduce photographs: Shutterstock: Andras Deak, 17, apple2499, 9, artemiya, 21, Eric Isselee, back cover, Jen Watson, 16, Julia Nikitina, 20 top, Keitma, 11, Sacha M, 15, slowmotiongli, cover, 19, Susan Flashman, 10, thanongsuk harakunno, 13, Vichy Deal, 20 bottom, Zeyad Mohamed Edriss, 14, Superstock: D. Parer & E. Parer-Cook/Minden Pictures, 5, Suzi Eszterhas/Minden Pictures, 6.

Printed and bound in India

Contents

Words in **bold** are in the glossary.

A TINY JOEY

Look at the tiny koala! A baby koala is called a **joey**. It grew inside its mother for about one month. Then it crawled into a **pouch** on her belly.

A baby koala has no fur. It cannot hear or see. But it can hold on to its mother. The mother koala can open and close her pouch using a special muscle. She keeps her baby from falling out.

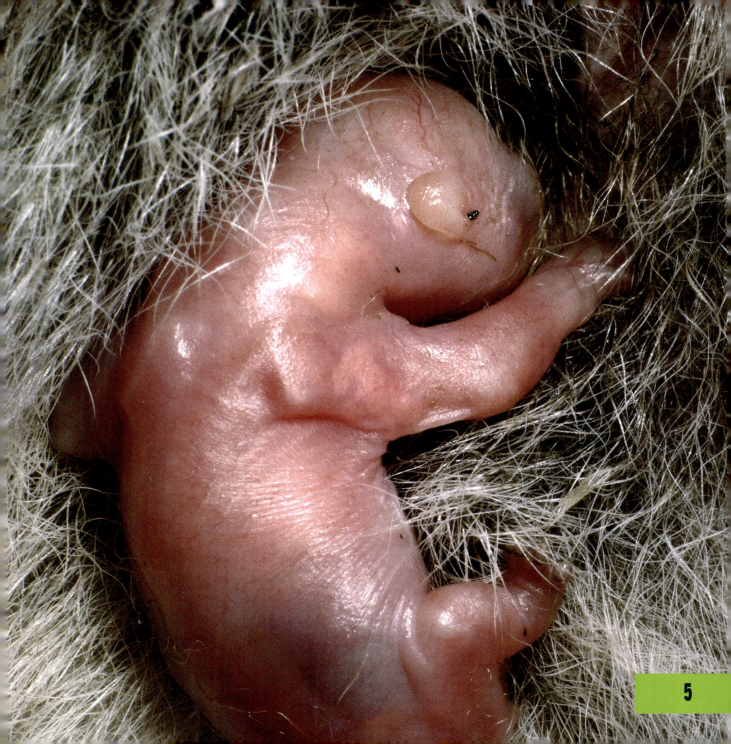

5

The baby koala lives in its mother's pouch for about six months. It drinks milk from its mother's body.

The joey slowly gets bigger. Fuzzy fur grows on its body. Ears form on its head. It opens its eyes and looks around. Then it pokes its head out of the pouch. The pouch is still its home.

LEAVING THE POUCH

The baby keeps growing. Sometimes it gets out of the pouch. But it stays close to its mother. It has strong claws. They help the baby grip on to its mother's back.

The joey goes back to the pouch to drink milk. It cuddles close to its mother to sleep.

Joeys stay with their mothers in a small area. This is called a home **range**. Other koalas live near by.

Koalas mark the trees in their areas. Their sharp claws scratch the bark. Male koalas sometimes put their scent on the trees. This tells other koalas not to eat from those trees.

KOALA FOOD

Adult koalas eat the leaves of **eucalyptus** trees. But the leaves are hard for their stomachs to break down. Young koalas must get their bodies ready to eat this food.

Baby koalas eat **pap**. It comes from their mother's bottoms. Pap looks and smells like runny poo. But eating pap will help the baby break down eucalyptus leaves.

Koalas are picky eaters. Their black noses sniff leaves. They carefully pick which leaves to eat. Mothers teach their young how to find the best leaves.

Koalas sleep for about 20 hours each day. They wake up to eat at night. Adult koalas eat about 0.5 kilograms (1 pound) of leaves each night.

LIFE IN THE TREES

Koala joeys grow up in the trees. They do not even get down to drink. They get water from the plants they eat.

A growing joey starts to explore the trees. But sometimes it wanders too far away. Then it makes a yipping sound. Its mother comes and finds it.

As joeys get bigger, extra fur grows on their bottoms. This makes sleeping in trees more comfortable.

ALL GROWN UP

After about six months, a joey is too big for its mother's pouch. The joey rides on its mother's back for up to one year. After a year, it stops drinking milk. It only eats leaves.

Joeys leave their mother after one to two years. The joey finds its own range.

A female koala is fully grown by about 2 years old. A male koala is fully grown by 3 to 4 years old.

MAKE YOUR MARK

Each koala has its own fingerprints, just like you do. Use your fingerprints to make a koala in its habitat.

What you need

- paper
- coloured pencils or felt-tip pens
- grey paint
- a paper plate

What you do

1. Draw a eucalyptus tree on the paper. Look back at the photos in this book to see what eucalyptus trees look like.

2. Pour a small amount of grey paint on the paper plate. Dip your fingers in the paint to make koalas in the trees. Your thumb can be its body, your pointing finger can be its head and your little finger can be its ears, legs and arms.

3. Let the paint dry.

4. Add black eyes, a nose and claws to your koala.

Glossary

eucalyptus kind of tree that koalas live in and eat the leaves of

joey young koala

pap runny waste from a mother koala that is eaten by her baby

pouch flap of fur on a female koala; a baby koala grows inside the pouch

range area where a koala and joey live together; several koalas can live within a range

Find out more

Books

Baby Koalas (Animal Babies), Jenna Grodzicki (Bearcub Books, 2021)

Koalas (Australian Animals), Sara Louise Kras (Raintree, 2019)

Websites

www.bbc.co.uk/newsround/51151597
This BBC Newsround video will teach you more about koalas.

www.dkfindout.com/uk/animals-and-nature/mammals/koala/
Learn more about koalas with DKFindout!

Index